Anything is Possible

By

Clifford E. Mendenhall

Once a

youngster

had a

disability

But

had

many

possibilities

Even

though

all we

go through

There is

nothing

we

can't do

As we

all grow

up and

cope

We hope

to have

lots of

support

and hopes

GOOD JOB

When

we all

begin

our

journey

in life

Many

opportunities

can come

to light

Sometimes

life will

throw

you a

curve ball

But nothing

can stop

you from

making it

through

it all

Through

all the

things

that may

go wrong

It's what

you go

through

that makes

you strong

Always

remember

through

all of

life's

challenges

Never

give up

and

always

keep your

head up

Library of Congress Registration Number: TXu002192222

ISBN: 9798558240689